Contents

Seed

An oak tree is a flowering
plant. It grows from a
seed called an acorn.
Acorns grow on an
oak tree every year.

4

Looking at Lifecycles

Oak Tree

Victoria Huseby

W
FRANKLIN WATTS
LONDON • SYDNEY

First published in 2007 by Franklin Watts
338 Euston Road, London NW1 3BH

Franklin Watts Australia
Level 17/207 Kent Street
Sydney NSW 2000

Editor: Rachel Tonkin
Designer: Proof Books
Picture researcher: Diana Morris
Literacy consultant: Gill Matthews
Science consultant: Andrew Solway

Picture credits:
Campbell/Topfoto: 15; Malcolm Forrow/Photographers Direct: 13;
Bob Gibbons/OSF: 4; Michael Gadomski/Photographers Direct: 9;
Duncan McEwan/NaturePL: 17, 19; Richard Packwood/OSF: front cover: 1, 21;
Gary K. Smith/FLPA: 7; Superbild/A1Pix: 11; Adrian Thomas/SPL: 5
Every attempt has been made to clear copyright.
Should there be any inadvertent omission please
apply to the publisher for rectification.

A CIP catalogue record for this book
is available from the British Library
ISBN: 978 0 7496 7108 2

Dewey Classification: 583'.46

Printed in Malaysia

Franklin Watts is a division of Hachette Children's Books.

5

Autumn

In Autumn, the acorns fall to the ground. Squirrels collect the acorns and bury some to eat during Winter. They forget where some of the acorns are, and these stay under the ground.

Root

Under the ground, the acorn begins to grow. A **root** grows out of the seed and down into the **soil**. The acorn contains a store of **energy** to help the root grow.

Shoot

A **shoot** then grows from the acorn up through the soil. The first leaves begin to appear.

11

Seedling

The **seedling**'s leaves take in energy from the Sun. This helps the seedling to grow bigger and bigger.

Young tree

After about 20 years, the seedling grows into a young oak tree. The tree has many branches. Every Spring, the branches are covered in new leaves.

Catkins

When the oak tree is about 20 years old, it begins to produce **flowers** each Spring. There are both male and female flowers. The male flowers are called **catkins**.

Acorns

Pollen from the catkins is blown by the wind on to the female flowers. The female flowers then become acorns.

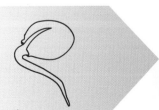

Ancient trees

Every Autumn, the leaves
of the oak tree fall off.
In Spring, new leaves grow.
The tree flowers and then
acorns appear again. Oak
trees can live to be over
1,000 years old.

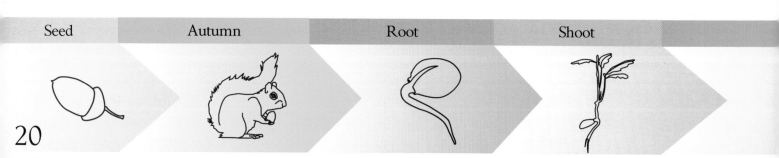

Seed Autumn Root Shoot

Seedling   Young tree   Catkins   Ancient trees

Oak tree facts

- Oak trees can grow to be over 40 metres high.

- Oak trees are more likely to be struck by lightning than any other tree.

- The oldest living oak tree is thought to be in Bulgaria, south-east Europe. The tree is about 1,650 years old.

- For every 10,000 acorns, only one will become an oak tree.

- An oak tree can take in over 200 litres of water a day through its roots.

Oak tree words

catkins
The fluffy flowers of an oak tree.

energy
The strength or power to do things, such as grow.

flowers
The colourful part of a plant in which the seed forms.

pollen
A powder found in the flowers of plants. Pollen must move from one plant to another for seeds to form.

root
The part of a plant that grows under the ground.

seed
The part of a plant that grows to make a new plant.

seedling
A young plant.

shoot
The first growth of a young plant above the ground. Shoot also means any new growth, such as a bud or branch, from a plant.

soil
The earth that plants grow in.

Index